Wicca for Beginners

A Starter Guide to Safely Practice & Understand the Secret of Magic ,Witchcraft, Spells, Rituals

# Introduction

The world of magic is full of immeasurable potential. There are literally thousands of spells in existence, for every purpose you could possibly imagine.

Of course, those who use magic as part of their practice of Wicca—and many other traditions of Witchcraft—will only work for positive or neutral purposes, never seeking to harm anyone or anything, and the spells in this book abide by this important rule.

In these pages you will find spells and other workings that, when applied with focused intention, can bring positive experiences into your life—and by extension, the lives of those you care about.

These spells cover a wide range of magical aims. Most are grouped into three categories: love and relationships, prosperity and abundance, and health and well-being, as these are the top three areas in life for which people tend to seek magical assistance.

However, they're not the only elements of the human experience, and that's why you'll find a sampling of other spells to give you just a hint of the possibilities for broadening your own magical practice.

In addition, this book covers a variety of magical approaches and techniques, from candle magic to divination to charms and other hand-made creations.

Each spell contains explicit instructions, but there are also opportunities to personalize many of the workings as you see fit.

If you're already fairly experienced in magic, you'll probably know first-hand that you can generally make substitutions for ingredients that are hard to acquire. If you're new, it's often helpful to follow spells as closely to the letter as you can until you cultivate a stronger connection to your intuition for improvising, but if your inner wisdom guides you to do something differently, by all means listen to it!

Of course, as flexible as magic can be, there are certainly some key steps and considerations that go into successful spellwork.

First and foremost, please note that the instructions for each of these spells assume that you have already charged your ingredients for the magical purpose you are pursuing.

Methods for charging tend to vary according to the type of object you're working with, but if you're not sure how to proceed, you can use a standard method that works for most anything: lay the object on an already-charged pentacle, preferably in direct sunlight or moonlight, and speak words of intention related to the spellwork you'll be doing. Depending on your practice, you might invoke the Goddess and God, the Elements, or other spiritual energies you work with.

If you're new to magic, research and try a few different methods for charging various tools, until you find what feels most appropriate for you.

Second, always remember that no matter the kind or quality of your ingredients, how well you charge them, or how well you follow the spell instructions to the letter, it is your state of mind that is the chief factor in any successful spellwork.

Approach a spell with doubt that it will work, and you've pretty much guaranteed that it won't. Approach it with anxiety, and you're likely to get mixed results or no results at all.

The most successful magic is done from a place of calm centeredness and with very focused intent. So always do whatever you need to do to get grounded, whether that's through meditation, visualization, breathing techniques, a ritual circle-casting, or all of the above. It is ultimately **your** energy that's shifting the reality of the Universe, so shape it well and use it wisely!

One way to help ensure that your energetic focus is aligned with a spell is to rewrite the spoken element in your own words. Of course, the words provided in these spells are already powerful and effective, but if you're inclined to be creative with language, you are invited to use words of your own.

Some Witches maintain that spells should rhyme, and there is definitely something to be said for the power that rhyme can lend to magic. Others find, however, that if a spell is too "sing-songy" it distracts them from speaking the words with authenticity and focus.

You'll find that some spells in this book make use of rhyme, while others do not. Try out some of each and see how you respond internally to the words, and again, feel free to tweak or completely rewrite them as you see fit.

A few more practical tips are worth mentioning here. Always work spells in a place where you know you'll be undisturbed by other people. Turn off your phone and do your best to create an ambience conducive to magic—whether that means music, incense, candles, etc.

Speaking of candles, always use caution, and never leave a burning candle unattended. If you're anointing a candle with oil, be sure to wipe excess oil from your fingertips before sparking that match or lighter—you don't want to mix skin and oil with fire!

Also, when it comes to spells containing herbs, keep in mind that the amounts listed are general suggestions—there's no need to measure out **exact** teaspoons or tablespoons, unless you find that doing so adds energy and focus to the spell. Otherwise, a rough estimation of the listed amount will do—as always, go with your gut instinct!

Finally, no matter how much, or how little, experience you have with spellwork, remember that there is always more room to learn and grow. Enjoy trying out these magical offerings, and if you wish, let them be a springboard of inspiration for creating your own spells. And don't forget to honor your results with love and gratitude.

## What Is Wicca?

If you go down to the woods today, you may have a big surprise. In deep forests and grass-clad clearings, you may find covens of Witches worshipping the ancient Pagan deities of their lands and peoples; chanting, drumming, feasting and rejoicing in the life that the Gods have given us. They may be making magic to heal the Earth or those that are sick; they may be practising the ancient arts of divination. They may be practising Wicca, the ancient art, craft and religion of Witchcraft.

Today, the words Wicca, Shamanism, Witchcraft, Witch, Wise Woman, Cunning Man, Magician are often heard; but what do they mean? Wicca is the religion of Witchcraft. Witchcraft is not merely a system of magic. Within the Wiccan community, Witchcraft has a capital letter and is used in a special sense. Wicca is a Pagan mystery religion of Goddess and God. It is also a Nature religion. It is not a remnant of the past and of the sixteenth- and seventeenth-century Witch trials. Ancient though the roots of this tradition are, it is alive and well in the world today.

My own Wiccan training was primarily in Britain, but since then I have worked with Witches in North America, Australia and all over Europe. Each country has its own Witchcraft traditions. These draw primarily on European traditions, but in the case of the United States, for instance, they are influenced by Native American spirituality and by West African traditions. Wicca is therefore a synthesis of a number of different belief systems that have endured into the modern age because they are relevant to our needs today.

The word Wicca itself is derived from the Anglo-Saxon word Wicce, a Witch. Originally this was pronounced Witcha but in modern times it is pronounced Wicka. The word Witch is a difficult one. It conjures images of the dark, the hag-like, the forbidden; the three Witches in William Shakespeare's play Macbeth; black candles, broomsticks, poisons, wax images with pins, incantations, 'hubble, bubble, toil and trouble', cauldrons, graveyards; many suspect things. There is also the image of the Witch as a vampire: a strong woman using her sexual energy to lure men into her power; just as in Greek myth the Witch Circe turned the hero Odysseus' men into swine.

Positive images of the Witch are more difficult to find, but they are there in folklore and children's stories. There is the user-friendly Granny - a nice elderly lady with silver-grey hair who lives in a cottage in the middle of the wood with a big black cat curled up by a warm fire. She is the Fairy Godmother whose magic wand heals all ills. There is the occasional TV Witch. Some people may remember or have seen re-runs of the television series Bewitched. This was one of my favourite television programmes as a child, but I could never see why the lovely Witch Samantha had married boring Darren or why she objected to doing housework by nose twitching. It seemed a very sensible idea to me.

Some Witch images are positive, others negative; but they have common threads. These give us the first clues on our quest to discover who and what Witches really are: the Witch is a magic-maker and Witches worship a Goddess - the Great Mother Goddess. They also worship the Horned God. In Greek mythology he is Pan and, to the Celts, Herne or Cernunnos. In other words, Witchcraft is a religion. It is a pre-Christian religion originating in the mists of time. It is based on remnants of simple Pagan traditions handed down in folklore and country custom. Onto these have been grafted more sophisticated beliefs from the more formal Paganisms of Rome, Greece and Egypt, and from the initiatory mystery traditions. Wicca involves the development of magical psychic powers; but hand in hand with the wisdom to use them. An initiatory system of spiritual development is an intrinsic part of the tradition.

## Who Are Today's Witches?

Who are they, these people who call themselves Witches, who walk the ancient ways, who work the traditional magics, who speak once more to long-silent Goddesses and Gods? They are men and women of all nations and races. They are young, old, rich, poor. They are those who have woken up to the fact that material creation is not the all and end all; that science does not have all the answers; nor do the so-called world religions. hey have remembered something which many of us have forgotten. Partly it is ancient wisdom; partly it is common sense.

People come to Wicca for many reasons. Some seek occult power and knowledge. Some are drawn to Wicca by feminism and the role of the Goddess; others by ecological awareness and reverence for Nature; still others seek spiritual transformation.

Magic is an attraction for some. Gerald Gardner, one of the 'founding fathers' or revivers of modern Wicca once wrote:

Witchcraft was, and is, not a cult for everybody. Unless you have an attraction to the occult, a sense of wonder, a feeling that you can slip for a few minutes out of the world into the world of faery, it is of no use to you.'

Many people come to Wicca because they already see themselves as Witches. We may have had a sense of an inner power that had no name; a sense that just beyond the realm of sight and sound and touch there dwelt another kingdom - the Land of Faery. Perhaps we went there in our dreams.

Some of us were aware that some of this Faery Power dwelt within us. Perhaps we had precognitive dreams, sometimes we knew the future. We may have tried to develop this by working with tarot cards and telling the fortunes of our friends. Perhaps we were scared when our predictions came true and stopped looking into the misty glass of the future. Perhaps we found we had the power of small magics. We could wish for something very hard and it would come true. Perhaps we found books of spellcraft on the shelves of our library or bookstore and tried them. Maybe when we talked to our relatives we found that some of our family had the sight. Perhaps our grandmother told fortunes using tea leaves, or our grandfather dreamt the family deaths the day before they occurred. Perhaps we had an aunt who was a medium, a grandfather who was a spiritual healer, a great grandmother who was a herbalist and cured the community in days when no one could afford a doctor unless someone was at death's door.

This heritage of power and sight may have been manifest in us from childhood, but we may have had no outlet for it; or perhaps it was discouraged. Perhaps it manifested in our teenage years, when often teenagers have what is called psychokinetic energy. Lights flicker when we walk by, photocopiers grind to a halt; vases mysteriously leap off shelves and smash themselves at our feet. Often our families have no explanations for these things, so we have to seek explanations elsewhere. Perhaps we come upon books of magic, tarot, astrology, divination, healing. We may find that the religious framework we were taught as children has no place for these arts, but there is a religious framework that does.

This is the religious framework of Wicca. In the early years of the Wiccan revival, most people came through the occult route; perhaps because other important aspects of Wicca were less well known. Today things are very different.

For women, Wicca is a spiritual path in which we can worship the Divine in its female form - as Goddess. Many women come to Wicca from feminism. They have re-evaluated the word Witch and realized that it involves the use of the innate powers of the Wise Woman. The Wise Woman was the traditional village midwife. (In French, midwives are still call sages femmes, wise women.) For those of you familiar with the tarot, the Wise Woman has affinity with the Queen of Pentacles – a very Earthy lady! Other women might consider the role of the Wiccan priestess attractive, allowing them to fulfil a spiritual role usually denied them in Western society today.

It is not only women who seek the Goddess. Men too are attracted by Wicca's vision of deity as both Goddess and God. In the popular mind, Witches are female and this can be a barrier to men interested in Wicca. However, both men and women are Witches. A male Witch is simply that - not a warlock or a wizard. The idea that Witches are always women is a relatively new one. At the height of the Witchcraft persecutions in Europe and America, both men and women were killed and when I came into Wicca in England a quarter of a century ago, there were more male than female Witches. It is more difficult for men to identify with the word Witch, but here are some ways of thinking about it. The traditional male Witch is a countryman. He is one who is in touch with the elements, who has worked the land, healed a bird's broken wing or the illness of a child; one who loves the Goddess and knows both Goddess and God, whatever any church might tell him.

Another route to Wicca is through the growing environmental awareness in society today. Wicca honours the Divine as manifest in Nature. The Earth is our spiritual mother and we sense that the Divine is not 'out there' but all around us. Nature itself is sacred and holy, a manifestation of the Divine Life Force. Greenpeace, environmental action, vegetarianism, animal rights, are all manifestations of a reawakening spirit of reverence towards the Earth. This was natural and instinctive to our ancestors, but recent centuries of urban living have suppressed it.

Initiation, in the sense of a personal transformatory experience of the Divine, is undoubtedly an attraction of Wicca for some. Some Wiccan traditions have three or more initiation ceremonies that mark transitions through spiritual change. Such rites can be powerful spiritual and psychological events that are life-enhancing and life-changing.

## Covens And Community

Unless you live in Salem, Massachusetts, site of the worst Witch persecutions in the United States and today centre of a thriving Witch tourist industry, you will not see Witches in black robes and pointed hats in your local supermarket. This is not because Witches prefer a diet of eye of newt and toe of frog, or that they do not do mundane things like shopping. However, for the most part, Witches today are much like everyone else; although they tend to be better educated than average. Some Witches are authors and teachers and spend all their time writing about and teaching the Craft; others are full-time healers or tarot readers. However, most Witches have conventional jobs. Certain professions attract Witches more than others. In the United States, information technology is popular; ironically the followers of the Old Religion are at the leading edge of high technology. In Europe, health care and social workers; artists, musicians and actors; and teachers and lecturers are the three biggest groupings.

Some Witches are solo Witches. Others belong to covens. Covens are stable groups of like-minded people who meet together to worship the Gods and do magic. They may also engage in social, environmental and teaching activities. The classic number of people in a coven is thirteen; more than this and groups become unwieldy and difficult to manage. However, many covens are smaller. Groups of five to nine can be very effective. Some are mixed sex groups; others cater for Witches who prefer single sex covens. Some Witches belong not to small covens but to training schools or coven networks which have hundreds of members. Whatever the size of the group though, it is important to remember that Wicca is not something which other people do for you, but something that you do for yourself. If we practise our Wicca solo that is obvious, but it is also the case in a group situation. Rites are participatory and emphasize the Divine within all.

Some Witches are trained by individual Witches and others come into Wicca through a coven operating an initiatory system. In some cases Witches come from Witch families, but most come from outside the tradition. They feel they are drawn to Wicca or are natural Witches seeking to make contact with teachers who can help them develop along the path. There are books through which it is possible to learn much. Books can add to our store of knowledge but it is difficult to learn Wicca from books alone. Learning Wicca is like learning anything else: at some stage we need to practise with others to improve our skill and knowledge and to assess how good we really are. Wicca is also a bit like learning a language. We can read books, listen to tapes, but in the end we need to speak that language with others to know how to use it.

Each coven has teachings derived from the accumulated generations who have worked in that particular coven. If it is part of an initiatory tradition, it will also have the core material of the tradition. This is recorded in a book of rites and spells, the Book of Shadows. Computers notwithstanding, each Witch must make his or her own handwritten copy. Wicca is part of the modem world, but it is also an inheritor of past traditions.

## Origins Of Wicca

Wicca's history is that of natural magic, the Pagan mystery traditions, such as those of Egypt and Eleusis, and of Celtic spirituality. Wicca draws on mysticism, astrology, runes, tarot and, in modem times, on insights from psychology. It also draws on the traditions of healing of body and of soul.

Although the Wiccan practice I describe here is European in origin, Wicca represents universal and fundamental beliefs and skills. Similar traditions exist all over the world; wherever native indigenous spirituality has not been suppressed. We find similar ideas in North America, South America, Africa, Asia, Polynesia, everywhere where people have sought to honour the Divine and to use the innate powers of the human psyche.

The Wiccan revival in the twentieth century began in England, sacred Albion, home of Glastonbury, Stonehenge and the legends of the Grail. This is perhaps no accident. The idea that the Western islands of Europe were Holy Ground and sacred soil is a long-held tradition. The greatest Druid training schools in the Celtic era were in Britain and Ireland. In Medieval times, scholars claimed that Britain was given to their ancestors by the Goddess Diana. In 1136,the historian Geoffrey of Monmouth described in his History of the Kings of Britain how refugees escaping in pre-Christian times from the siege of Troy were desperately seeking a new homeland.

Their leader called upon Diana to help them:

O powerful Goddess,

terror of the forest glades,

yet hope of the wild woodlands,

you, who have the power to go in orbit,

through the airy heavens and the halls of hell,

pronounce a judgement which concerns the Earth.

Tell me which lands you wish us to inhabit.

Tell me of a safe dwelling-place

where I am to worship you down the ages,

and where, to the chanting of maidens,

I shall dedicate temples to you.

This he said nine times; four times he proceeded round the altar, pouring the wine which he held upon the sacrificial hearth; then he lay down upon the skin of a hind which he had stretched before the altar. Having sought for slumber, he at length fell asleep.
It was then about the third hour of the night, when mortal beings succumb to the sweetest rest; that it seemed to him the Goddess stood before him and spoke these words to him:

Brutus, beyond the setting of the Sun,

past the realms of Gaul,

there lies an island in the sea,

once occupied by giants.

Now it is empty and ready for your folk.

These Pagan links are part of the reason why Witchcraft has revived most quickly in England rather than in other parts of Europe. Another is England's remoteness from Rome. This meant that it was Christianized later than some parts of Europe and with the Protestant Reformation could more easily break from Rome. English Protestantism was not a fanatical variety. It did not engage in Witch persecutions with the same enthusiasm as some of its Catholic and Protestant neighbours. English Protestantism was a curious hybrid of moderate Catholicism and Lutheranism in a church headed not by a religious figure but by the monarch - the King or Queen. This Church of England was a state church whose interests were as much about creating a stable society as about religion.

On the fringes of Western Europe many Pagan ideas endured in ways they could not elsewhere. Other than Celtic Brittany in North-west France, Britain and Ireland are the parts of Europe where Pagan sacred sites have best survived. Scottish, Welsh, English and Irish cultures all show their Pagan origins. Scratch the surface and you will find village customs such as May-pole dancing, well-dressing, the Abbots Bromley Horn Dance, Morris Men, Harvest festivals - all remnants of Pagan religious customs.

People often think of Europe as having being Christian for two thousand years, but this is not the case. Paganism and Christianity were still struggling over a thousand years later. Medieval laws tell us much about Paganism because they tell us what it was necessary to suppress. This included making offerings to non-Christian Gods, performing Witchcraft or divination, swearing vows at wells, trees or stones, and gathering herbs with non-Christian incantations. In the eleventh century when King Canute issued laws against Heathenism or Paganism, this is what he forbade.

## We earnestly forbid every Heathenism:

Heathenism is, that men worship idols;

that is, that they worship Heathen Gods,

and the Sun or the Moon,

fire or rivers,

water-wells or stones,

or forest trees of any kind;

or love Witchcraft.

Witchcraft and Paganism survived in rural areas as part of the folk traditions and folk medicine of the people. This does not mean that the ruling classes of society were not exposed to these folk traditions. Communal festivities such as May Day were celebrated by both high and low.

Witches were consulted by all strata of British society well into the nineteenth century. Hannah Green of Yeadon in Yorkshire, known as the 'Ling Bob Witch', inherited her mother's practice which she ran for forty years. In 1810, she left a thousand pounds in her will, an enormous sum of money in those days. Cunning Murrell, who died in 1860, was a male witch from Essex who practised healing, averting the evil eye, astrology, herbalism, and spellcraft for clients as far away as London. After his death he was found to have owned a trunkful of books and manuscripts including magical texts from the seventeenth century.

Witchcraft and Pagan religious traditions survived in rural areas, but Witchcraft would have remained an underground tradition if it was not for the work of one man, Gerald Gardner, who became familiar to many thousands of people through his radio broadcasts, books and media publicity. He was one of the first Witches in the twentieth century to talk publicly about his beliefs and to share them with others. Most photographs show him in later life, with a white goatee beard looking for all the world like an elderly Pan. Gerald Gardner spent most of his adult working life away from Europe in far flung outposts of the British Empire. He was able to study and get to know the indigenous peoples and further his interest in folklore, naturism, Pagan religions and Witchcraft. When Gerald Gardner retired to England in the 1930s, he made contact with a coven of English Witches. These Witches met in the New Forest, an ancient royal hunting ground of the Norman kings in southern England. The coven had a system of initiation not dissimilar to the three degrees of Freemasonry. The group practised spell-making, ritual and worship. Their rituals celebrated a seasonal myth cycle. Just how ancient the tradition was is a subject of much debate. Nevertheless, Gerald Gardner's two most well known books Witchcraft Today (1954) and The Meaning of Witchcraft (1959) produced a huge surge of interest, inspiring a movement that has spread around the world.

# Getting Familiar: Different types of Wicca

Before we move on to the principles of Wicca, I thought it right to first look at the different branches of Wicca since we keep on reliving the fact that Wicca has many branches.

## Alexandrian Wicca

We touched on this in passing. Alexandrian Wicca has its roots firmly in the 1960s with Alex Sanders as its father. For this reason, he, Alex Sanders, has earned the title of the 'king' of the witches. There are those who speculate that the rituals in the Alexandrian Wicca come from the Gardnerian Wicca.

## British Wicca

The British Wicca is a mix of Gardnerian and Celtic Wicca. The most famous organization or coven that practices British Wicca is the International Red Garters. The practice mostly moves within the Farrar studies, who are a famous witch wife and husband from England. Like most Wiccans, the British Wiccans practice a degree process and have a structured belief system. The covens that practice this type of Wicca bear the name Co-ed.

## Celtic Wicca

The Celtic Wicca is a mix of the Gardnerian/Druidic pantheon Wicca. It stresses the use of the elements, nature, and the ancient ones. Celtic Wiccans then and now have vast knowledge in the use of stones and plants for magical and healing purposes. They also respect and believe in fairies, gnomes, and their magical healing powers.

## Caledonii Wicca

The Caledonii Wicca bore the name Hecatine tradition. Its origin is Scottish and still preserves the unique festival of the Scots to date.

## Ceremonial Witchcraft Wicca

Covens that follow the doctrines of the Ceremonial Witchcraft Wicca use a lot of ceremonial magic in their practice. They integrate Egyptian magic and ritual into their practice. They also favor Qabbalistic magic.

## Dianic Wicca

The Dianic Wicca has its bearings in 1921 from Margaret Murray who pointed it out. The practice integrates vari

ous traditions. However, the most common one is of the goddess. For this reason, the Dianic Wicca has adopted a feministic approach.

## Eclectic Wicca

The Eclectic Wicca indicates that its practitioner does not follow a particular tradition, denomination, or magical practice. The practitioner learns and adopts many magical systems if they work best for them. It is therefore the most common form of modern Wicca.

## Gardnerian Wicca

We have covered the Gardnerian Wicca to a degree.

## Hereditary Witch Wicca

Those who practice this type of Wicca can trace their practice of the religion backwards through their family tree. Most of them have a fair understanding of the Old religion taught to them by relatives living during the era of the Old religion.

## Kitchen Witch Wicca

This type of Wicca has done its fair share of runs around the mill. One who practices this type of Wicca does so by hearth and home; he or she deals with the practical part of the religion. He or she also relies heavily on magic, the elements, and the earth.

## Pictish Witchcraft Wicca

Pictish Witchcraft is a form of Scottish witchcraft that employs all aspects of animals, minerals, nature, and vegetables. It is mainly magical in nature and less religious.

## Pow-Wow Wiccan

Pow-Wow Wiccan is native to South Central Pennsylvania. It is less of a religion and more of a system with a base from a 400-year-old Elite German magic. Today, the system has deteriorated to a faith healing one.

## Seax-Wicca

This type of Wicca came from Raymond Buckland in 1973. The tradition is acceptable to most Wiccans because it integrates many magical aspects and practices.

## Solitary witch Wicca

A solitary Wiccan is one who practices alone. To some extent, there is a belief that at one point a solitary witch Wiccan was part of a coven but decides to extricate him or herself.

## Strega Witch Wiccan

The Strega witch Wiccan has its roots in Italy at around 1353 from a woman called Aradia. Today, this group of Wiccans is by far the smallest in terms of numbers in the US.

## Teutonic Witch Wiccan

There is a belief that Teutons are mainly from German speaking regions. This type of Wicca is also known as the Nordic tradition.

With that in mind, we can now look at the guiding principles of Wicca as a practice. I should also point out that these principles are synonymous with all branches of Wicca practice despite the branch, tradition, and doctrine.

# The Altar

There is a lot that goes into an altar. It's more than just a few pieces of wood or rocks and some candles. An altar is your divine connection with the God and Goddess and should represent everything about you and what you want to accomplish. It is the most personal tool any Wiccan will utilize, and it is an ever-changing instrument.

To get started with your altar, you must first understand the elements and what they represent. At the end of this chapter, I will give you an example of a set-up of an altar.

## The Elements

The five elements play a crucial role in Wiccan belief systems. Notice that I said five and not four. There are four commonly known elements, but the fifth one that some Wiccans choose to believe in and others do not. For information purposes, all five will be explained.

### Air

Air is the element of the mind. Its directions are south and east and its colors are sky blue and yellow. This element is masculine and associated with the God, yet its seasons are spring and summer. Zodiac signs for this element are Gemini, Libra, and Aquarius, and the tools commonly associated with the element are an athame, blade, sword, and incense. Therefore, you should have one of these tools at your altar to represent air.

In addition to one of the tools, you can have feathers as birds represent the air element, or you can choose a stone with sky blue or yellow coloring. Most Wiccans choose items they find as they're walking through nature.

### Earth

This element represents the physical plane and is the element of the Goddess. Colors associated with this element are green, brown, black and tan, and the direction is north. Zodiac signs include the Taurus, Virgo, and Capricorn. Tools for this element include stones, crystals, salt, soil, the pentacle, mirrors, shields, and coins. Earth is the element of fertility and healing, as well as the body and comfort. Most Wiccans choose a little bit of soil from an area that has meaning for them to put on their altar.

You may also choose stones that represent Earth and crystals. Just be sure that whatever you chose has meaning to you as this is your personal connection to the divine.

### Fire

Fire is associated with the spiritual plane and our emotions. Its colors are red and orange and its direction is east or south. Fire is a masculine element commonly associated with passion, intuition, light, power, sexuality, desire, and the soul. Zodiac signs include Aries, Leo, and Sagittarius. Candles, wands, and blades are associated with this element. Most Wiccans choose a candle that has meaning for them to represent the fire element on their altar, but you may also choose an athame or a stone that represents fire.

## Water

The element of water is associated with the astral or emotional plane and the western direction. Its colors are aqua, blue, sea green and black. Water is a feminine element and often associated with the Goddess. Zodiac signs include Cancer, Scorpio, and Pisces and tools include the chalice, bowl, caldron, and shell. You may choose to place a clean, blessed bowl of water on your altar or perhaps something from the ocean such as a seashell.

## Spirit

The fifth element that is made of all the other elements and creates them at the same time, spirit, is the element of the divine. Its directions are the center, above and below and its signs are all the zodiac signs. Spirit represents the universe and all that it holds. Its tools included the caldron and pentacle, and it represents harmony, unity, creation, centering, unconditional love, and sacredness. Everything that you place on your altar represents spirit.

## Your Altar

You may be wondering why you should even build an altar in the first place. It seems archaic and a little outdated, but our ancestors did know a thing or to when it came to practicing. An altar is your personal connection to the divine and every day, when you sit down and look at your altar, you will be reminded of what you are practicing and what it stands for. You will have an immense feeling of unconditional love and understand when you are in tune with your altar. It is merely a symbol of whom you are and why you exist, but don't underestimate the physical presence of an altar.

Therefore, you should build an altar whether you believe it is silly or not. At some point, you will come to understand the importance of this physical symbol of your love and your religion.

So how do you set up an altar?

You'll need several things:

- One or several items to represent each element that you have found through your travels or that resonate with you in some way. For example, one woman used a steel tile as the base of her altar. To anyone else, it was just a tile, but to her, it was a symbol of unconditional love. A special friend had told her he loved her on that tile, and so it symbolized the base of her altar as love.

- A compass to tell you the directions so that everything is placed in its correct spot.

- Your understanding and acceptance of the God and Goddess.

Once you have those three things, you should set up your altar as follows:

- Traditional altars face either east or north, but as you start to decipher which elements most sing to your soul, you will choose your own altar direction. Do what feels natural.

- Next, place a white or black cloth on your altar table or spot and place a candle in the center. Lighting the candle is your symbol of being closer to the God and Goddess.

- If you have any items and you know which element they belong to, you may place accordingly:

- **Air to the east**
- **Water to the west.**
- **Earth to the north.**
- **Fire to the south.**

- Any crystals, stones or other objects you are unsure of can be placed anywhere on your altar until you better understand them and can place them where they belong. Follow your intuition.

- Another way to find excellent tools and objects to place on your altar is to look into your ancestry. Try to find items that resonate with your bloodlines as these are more powerful to you.

# Wiccan Tools Commonly Found on the Altar

Now that you have your altar set up, you're going to need some tools in order to perform the rituals. The following is a list and a description of each item you should have on your altar. Be sure to place it in the correct spot for the best effect!

## Athame

Pronounced Ah-tha-may, athames are traditionally a black-handled knife; however, it doesn't have to be metal. It can be carved from wood or stone as it's not meant to cut anything in the physical plane, but only the astral plane. The athame finds its home in the East and should be placed on the east side of the altar. These knives hold the yang or God energy and are associated with the masculine. They're usually used to cut energetic ties in rituals.

## Bell

Bells are akin to the voice of the Goddess and they're used to bring Her attention to you and vice versa. They're used to clear out negative energy during a ritual and to bring about healing and loving energy at the end of a ritual.

## Direction Candles

Candles on an altar are meant to invoke and hold the power of each direction. Thus, you should have color coded candles on your altar. Your candles for the north should be black, green or brown. Candles for the East should be yellow or white. For the south, red or orange, and for the west they should be blue or aqua.

The center candle should either be a white and black pair or a white, silver or gold candle to represent the divine.

## God and Goddess Candles

These candles can be found in the center of the altar or they can be found along the edges. You can use pillar candles, one black and one white, to represent the God and Goddess in the center. If you're performing a ritual that is more in tune with the God, you should use just one black candle. If you're performing a ritual more in tune with the Goddess, you can choose to use a white, gold or silver candle or you can use three candles – white, red and black – to represent the Maiden, Mother, and Crone.

## Chalice

The chalice is one of the most important tools on the altar. It represents the Mother Goddess and is the yin on the altar. You can choose to have a very fancy chalice with jewels encrusted on it or you can use something as simple as a silver chalice. Silver is representative of the light and the Goddess, so silver is perfectly acceptable to use for your chalice. Pretty much anything that is round and curvy, even a bowl, is a good tool to use as a chalice.

## Deities

It is not necessary to have a statue of any particular deity on your altar, but you may choose to have a representative of the God or Goddess you have chosen to follow or more than one. These are more than just a reminder of the deity on the altar, they are a physical vessel where you can channel the divine presence of the God or Goddess directly to your altar. Your altar will become a living temple where the Divine dwells if you choose to have a statue of a deity on it.

## Libation Dish

The libation dish is a bowl or a cup in the center of your altar that will receive your offerings to the God and Goddess. You may use your chalice or a caldron for this purpose if you have limited space. When you're finished with your libation dish, you should discard the contents by burying them in the earth or allowing them to float down a river or stream. This allows them to be carried to the Divine.

## Offerings

Your offerings will be placed into your libation dish. These are gifts of thanks and prayer that you may bring to your altar for the God and Goddess. Flowers are usually kept on the altar as an offering, yet anything beautiful or special to you is a good item to offer. Offerings should not be anything that could harm another thing, so flowers are usually the optimal choice. In addition, be sure it's nothing that will pollute the ground or water when you discard of them when you're finished.

## Pentacle

The most commonly misunderstood symbol of the Wiccan belief system is the pentacle. It is often confused with the pentagram, an upside down, five-point star within a circle. The pentacle is an **upright** five-pointed star within a circle and is usually placed in the center of the altar. The pentacle is one of the most important altar tools as it provides protection and power by drawing the five elements together.

## Salt Water

You can place this inside your chalice or your caldron at the center of the altar if you find your space is limited. Salt and water are not only used in the physical world for cleansing, but also in the energetic realm, too. Salt represents the energies of the earth and water uniting and the ocean womb that gave birth to all life on this planet. It may seem insignificant at first, but it represents so much more than just a little salt in water. It is the representation of life.

### Feather

Feathers or sometimes incense are used to represent air and should be placed in the east. They are used to cleanse an area energetically and call in certain powers. Feathers and incense should be chosen according to the type of ritual being performed.

### Stones and Crystals

These are commonly used to represent the earth and should be placed to the north. Each stone and crystal has its own meaning.

### Wand

The wand is a masculine tool and represents yang. It should be placed in the south to represent power and will. Your wand can be made of any natural material. Wood is traditional, but it can be made of anything you'd like. Each type of wood has a different meaning, so be sure to research the type of wood you would like for your wand.

### Broom

The broom is not really an altar tool, but it is used to dispense of negative energy in a sacred space. You should have them nearby your altar space and use them before and after you perform a ritual in order to cleanse the area.

### Cauldron

They were traditionally cast-iron and large, but they come in all sizes now and can be as small as a ramekin. They're handy for burning your incense or herbs and is one of the reasons they're a common altar tool.

### Working Knife

If you have a wooden or stone athame, you may need to keep a working knife at your altar in case you need to cut anything. Your working knife should be white handled.

### Book of Shadows

Your book of shadows can be any book that has your spells and rituals written down. You're no expected to remember everything that you have learned, and a book of shadows can come in handy when you're in doubt about a ritual you're performing. At best, your book of shadows should be kept on your altar, but if you do not want to leave it there for privacy reasons, you should place it underneath the altar or in another sacred area.

Those are some of the most common items you will find on an altar, but almost every altar has an individual's unique items on it, too. Remember, this will be your most sacred place and should represent everything about you. If you find you resonate with one element over the others, you may want to have more of that item on your altar. Set it up until you are comfortable with how it looks.

## Law of Threefold

The Wiccan Rede represents the ethical code of the people who follow the Wicca path. This is the Wicca version of 'The law of cause and effect'.

The term "Rede" originates from the old English word "roedan" which means to direct, or to lead. The Wiccan Law of three was written in the beginning of the 20th century by an unknown source.

Wicca teaches that we all send energy into the Universe with our words and actions, and whatever energy we sent out, we get it back threefold. Wiccans believe in the right to use their will and energy freely as long as it does not cause harm to another human being. The Law of Three has directs the physical, emotional and spiritual world of the follower. Wiccans believe that, ultimately, everyone is responsible for his or her actions and doings. Trying to gain power over other people and achieving your goals at the expense of someone else is strictly prohibited in Wicca. They do not worship nor believe in Satan and human sacrifices are not part of this religion. Those who practice black magic and try to gain power over other people, try to harm other people are not considered Wiccan.

## Sabbats

The Sabbats and Esbats are the actual events in Nature. Sabbats are based on the solar calendar and they celebrate The God and The Sun as the male energy of The All. Sabbats refer to the natural cycles of the Earth. There are eight Sabbats and they represent the equinoxes - the two days in the year when the day and the night are of equal duration, the longest and the shortest day of the year, the longest night of the year also known as the solstice and the midpoints between these natural manifestations.

The Sabbats which represent the midpoints between these four occurrences represent the peaks of the four seasons. They are called the major Sabbats.

### Samhain: October 31

Also known as Halloween or the Witch's New Year. This is one of the most important holidays in Wicca, and it represents a major spiritual event. On this day they honor the dead, as it marks the death of the Lord. It is said that on this day the veil between the living and the dead is thinnest. On this day, they leave food out for loved ones who died.

Yule: December 21 Winter solstice

Represents the longest night of the year. The God is reborn again and the light is returned to Earth. They celebrate this holiday by exchanging gifts as a symbol for better future.

Imbolc: February 2

Also knows as Brigid's day-keeper of the sacred fire. Imbolc represents the peak of the winter, and it is celebrated through lighting fires and candles.

Ostara: March 21

Symbolizes the beginning of Spring, new life, and fertility. It hold the religious significance of Nature's rebirth and is considered as the time for new projects and personal development. Wiccans celebrate this with boiled eggs and blessings for a better future.

Beltane: May 1st

Represents the peak of Spring and is celebrated as the day when God and Goddess unite in a sacred marriage. Beltane is inspired by the rebirth of life, green nature, and blossoming of trees and flowers. It is a great day for bringing flowers to your home.

Summer Solstice: June 21: A midsummer

The start of the summer and the longest day of the year. This is a great period to perform healing magick, especially through outdoor rituals. Nature in this period is most abundant.

Lughnassad: August 2: First harvest

Characterizing the beginning of the full harvest, Lughnassad is also known as the Feast of Bread and is traditionally the day for baking bread. While performing rituals, Wiccans decorate their altar with fruits and vegetables.

Mabon: September 21 Harvest festival

The length of the day and the night is equal and it marks the approach of winter and darkness. During this time, Wiccans celebrate and give thanks to God for the abundance received that year.

## Esbats

Esbats are Moon rituals through which Wicca celebrate the Goddess and the feminine energy. Esbats celebrations usually worship the full moon and it is believed that on the full moon the magickal powers of the Goddess are at their peak.

At least once a month Wiccans and Witches honor the Goddess by celebrating one of the three phases of the moon, depending on what kind of energy they need for themselves.

- New Moon

Wiccans perform rituals on new moon when they need a new beginning, a fresh start in their lives.

- The Waxing Moon

This is the time of the year when the illuminated part of the moon is growing bigger and brighter. It is considered the ideal time to gain more positivity and strength in your life for all the new goals you've set for yourself under the new moon.

-The Full Moon

This is the time when Moon's energy is at its peak. This is the time to cast your spells and go for what you truly want. The three days before and after the Full Moon are considered a period of great power and influence as the night of the full moon.

-The Waning Moon

This is the period when the moon is getting smaller and it represents the perfect time to get rid of all the negativity in your life. This negativity can come in any shape or form; however, it is important to note that no one must be harmed in this process.

A solar year has 13 full moons, the 29.5-day lunar cycle 1, a year has one full moon per month plus one extra called the Blue Moon.

### January: Wolf Moon

This is the time for self - evaluation. See yourself as a seed that has been planted and is waiting for the spring to be born again.

### February: Storm Moon

A perfect time to get rid of any negativity. The full moon signifies self - forgiveness, mental house cleaning, and self - purification.

### March: Chaste Moon

A great time for new beginnings and to start working on the projects you planned last fall and set your ideas to cultivate.

### April: Seed Moon

It is time for fertility, wisdom, and growth. A perfect time to saw the seeds of your magick. Move from planning into action.

### May: Hare Moon

A celebration of health, life, romance and loving relationships. Great time to embrace your true self and make some time living your own passion.

### June: Dryad Moon

Known as Strawberry Moon, it represents the Lover's full moon that gives energy for love, marriage and success. A time to nurture your inner garden.

### July: Mead Moon

A great time for meditation, dream work and prosperity. Performing magick in this period of the year is an especially sublime experience.

### August: Wyrt Moon

Perfect time to reap the benefits from your magick work and thank the God and the Goddess for the abundance received, crafts and ambition.

### September: Harvest Moon

Time for protection and prosperity. A perfect time to reorganize your spiritual and emotional state from summer.

### October: Blood Moon

Use the moon's energies for setting new goals, enhance your spiritual life, meditate on death and rebirth and think about reincarnation.

### November: Snow Moon

A good time to work on yourself, to reduce stress and to gain strength for your relationships with others.

### December: Oak Moon

It is the last full moon of the year. Plan what you want to achieve for the next year and ask Goddess for guidance.

# Perfect Time for Doing Magick

When we think of magick, the image in front of our eyes is usually one of performing night time rituals. But as I stated before, Wiccan God is represented by the Sun and Sunlight. You are free to perform a ritual when you feel the time is perfect for you, whether it is during the day or at night.

### Magick ritual at Dawn

Dawn itself is a magickal period of the day, a time when the day is slowly waking up and the sky is half bright half dark. It is the perfect time for new ideas, new beginnings, and spiritual rebirth. In the past, witches collected plants at dawn to make love potions.

### Sunrise magick ritual

Everything is awakened. The Sun is up and its light is growing stronger. When you wake up in the morning, do not forget to recall your dreams and to do meditation for at least five minutes to refresh your energy. This is a perfect time of the day to cast spells for achieving your goals and to get rid of your bad habits. You can cast a spell to stop smoking or lose weight. Place your oracle or tarot cards and visualize the day that follows.

### Magick ritual at Noon

The energy of the God is at its peak and it is most powerful during this period. There is an enormous amount of energy to use for your magick. Use this energy to gain strength and work on issues you feel you need to overcome

### Magick ritual at Dusk

The light of the day is near the end and the darkness of the night is slowly approaching. This is the time when the gates of the magickal world are wide open, and performing magick rituals during this period will grant you full access to these worlds. Communication with Divine energies is especially strong.

### Nighttime magick ritual

The energy of the Goddess is very strong at night. Now you can reflect on the day that passed and concentrate only on the positive experiences. You can use this energy to cast a spell and call more positive things in your life.

Midnight magick ritual

    Also known as Witch Hour represents the perfect time to connect with Goddess and to soak in the energy of the Moon. This is a great time to tap into your intuition and your inner world. Perform a ritual and cast a spell to banish the negativity around you and to gain the healing energy of the Universe. Light a candle in honor of the Goddess and be silent. Only then can you hear her wise words. Ask for her guidance and help, ask her to join you in your life and as the moon shines bright ask the Lady to light your path. This is the time when you feel and embrace her strong presence.

## Thought Forms and Magic

Of course, Witches and others who practice magic know that there are strategies we can put in place to raise our vibrational frequency to a level that allows what we desire to come into our lives. Through spellwork, we can intentionally release negative thought forms and even create positive ones to more deliberately manifest our intended outcomes.

We'll offer a few examples of such workings below, but first let's take another look at the practice of magic with this concept of thought forms in mind.

Once you accept that thought takes form, and that the more energy a thought form receives, the more powerful it becomes, then you can begin to see **spells themselves** as thought forms. Indeed, all magic can be viewed as the directed use of thought forms.

In this framework, successful "tried and true" magical methods are successful because they have been used many times by many different people over time—in some cases, for centuries. In other words, the repeated focus on a particular ritual, incantation, or set of ingredients has, over time, made it more and more powerful.

For example, consider the various systems of magical correspondences discussed in Part Two, some of which date back to ancient times.

It's likely that after any given correspondence—such as the magical properties of a plant or a color—was first observed or intuited, it was then tested, confirmed and communicated to other magical practitioners. In this way, through the passing on of magical lore, the thought form containing the knowledge of the correspondence spread and strengthened with each new instance of attention to it and use of it in magic.

So when we use the color red to manifest an experience involving passion, for example, we're drawing on the energy of centuries of years of experience, and connecting with that very powerful universal thought form on the spiritual plane.

For example, as mentioned in Part Two, if the words of a particular spell don't resonate with you, it will be hard to say them in a way that will "convince" the Universe that you truly desire the thing that you're affirming. In this case, it's best to adapt the spell in a way that feels most true to your own self, and/or create your own spells from scratch.

Of course, this is easier said than done if you're just starting out. If you're new to magic, you may need to try various kinds of spells to get a sense for what you're most comfortable with. As you gain experience, you can start using spells from sources you trust as templates for your own unique spells, until eventually you have your own particular style of magic, relying on your own tried and true thought forms to manifest the changes you desire in your life.

The following spells and rituals provide concrete methods for working with thought forms to achieve a better state of mind for working successfully with the Law of Attraction.

The first two offerings are aimed at clearing unwanted negativity and eliminating old, well-entrenched thought forms from your consciousness. These are fairly simple and can be performed by anyone at any level of experience with magic.

The third spell is somewhat more advanced, and requires more practice in meditation and visualization to be truly effective. If you're new to magic, you may want to work with more basic spells for a while before giving this one a try.

## A Sacred Circle Energy Cleansing

Thought forms are actually visible to some clairvoyant people, who can see them with their "third eye." This skill is often used in energy healing, where unwanted thought forms, which appear as dark or dingy "spots" on the aura, are detected and then removed from the affected person's energy field.

The visualization in this ritual draws on the same concept, but you do not have to be practiced at "seeing" auras to experience the benefits.

Doing this work within a circle of sea salt adds extra effectiveness—the salt's purifying qualities will enhance the clearing, while its protective qualities will seal out any stray or unwanted energy while the spell is underway. For even more powerful effects, try working this spell when the moon is waning.

Before you begin, it's best to take a ritual cleansing bath, which will give you an energetic "head start" on the clearing process. You can add sea salt, calming essential oils, and/or herbs to the bath to create a soothing transition from your everyday "reality" into a magical, healing mindset. (If you don't have a bathtub, a nice hot shower will also do the trick.)

**You will need:**
- 1 white candle
- 1 smudge stick and a bowl of soil or loose smudging herbs and a fire-proof dish (**Note:** White sage is considered to be the best traditional herb for energetic clearing work, but you can also use Silver King artemisia (a related plant), cedar, rosemary, or lavender.)
- 1 feather (optional)
- Sea salt

**Instructions:**

After your ritual bath (or shower), gather your ingredients and place them in the center of what will be your circle, whether this is on your altar or the floor. Open a window (at least a crack) so the old, unwanted energy will have somewhere to go, rather than lingering around in your space.

Light the candle, then mark your circle with a solid line of salt, affirming as you do so that you're creating a sacred circle where only positive energy exists.

**If you like, you can say** "All that is wanted stay in; All that is unwanted jump out," **or similar words.**

From the center of the circle, ignite the smudging herbs.

Use the feather or your dominant hand to wave the smoke all around your body, starting at your feet and moving upward. Be sure to fan the smoke behind yourself as well, so that you fully clear your energy field.

As you work, visualize your body filling with light, and repeat the following or similar words:

"As I stand in my full power, I send all negative energy out of my being and bring forth Universal light in its place."

If your third eye picks up any "dusty" or grey areas, visualize them leaving your body and dissolving as they float out the opened window.

Once you've reached the top of your head, keep going for about another foot.

When you're finished, allow the smudging herbs to smolder out on their own (if using a smudge stick, lay it gently in the bowl of soil).

Sweep up and discard the salt.

You should now feel calm, clear, and receptive to positive energy.

## "Starving" Stubborn Thought Forms

For routing out more persistent negative thought forms—those which are usually self-created and highly disturbing or annoying—the most effective methods involve simply refusing to "feed" them with any more energy.

To do this, you need to introduce alternative thought forms and/or actions to focus on instead.

Here are a few possibilities to try whenever a negative thought or feeling sneaks up on you:

- Sweep your dominant hand across your forehead and "pull" the thought from your brain, then fling it far from your body. Visualize it flying out of the Earth's atmosphere and being obliterated by the heat of the Sun.
- Say to it in a cheerful voice, **"No thanks, not interested. Please transmute to light."** Imagine closing a door on it before it can enter your inner space.
- For particularly disturbing, fear-based thoughts, visualize a globe of golden light surrounding the thought and evaporating it. Say **"I neutralize this energy and transform it into love and light."**

You may have to repeat your chosen method several times over a long period of time, but eventually you will starve the thought form out of existence, just as an unwanted salesperson will eventually stop knocking on your unanswered door.

If something is particularly bothersome or interfering, you might consider consulting a professional energy healer who can help you speed things along.

## A Directed Thought Form Spell

Although the majority of what we call "thought forms" are largely unintentionally or unconsciously created, you can also **purposefully** create a thought form and send it forth into the Universe to achieve an intended aim.

The key is to be clear and specific in the creation of the thought form. It's a bit like programming a robot to complete a specific task for you—if you don't describe exactly what you need done, it may not get done correctly, or at all!

Be sure your mind is clear and calm—do not create and program a thought form when you're feeling actively anxious about achieving your aim, or your "assistant" will be confused by the negative energy you're putting into it, whether you mean to or not.

If you just can't seem to clear your mind, try meditating for at least 15 minutes before working the spell. Incense or essential oil in a diffuser can also be very helpful for shifting into the necessary psychic state. For incense, you might try frankincense, patchouli, or nag champa. Essential oils of cinnamon, lavender, or sandalwood are also good choices, but in either case, go with what works best for you.

One important thing to note about intentionally created thought forms is that they will not simply "disappear" on their own completely, even if you forget about them. That's why it's recommended that you instruct the thought form to dissolve either when the manifestation has occurred, or after a specified amount of time passes.

Many Witches recommend no longer than 7 days, as eventually the thought form can lose its focus and/or collect energetic "dust," complicating or even thwarting your results.

(**Note:** if you don't see results within 7 days, don't automatically assume your spell didn't work. It may be that it simply takes longer for the results to manifest in your experience, so you might want to give it a bit more time before trying again.)

You will need:

- Incense (or essential oil) of your choice
- 1 white spell candle (or color associated with your specific aim)
- Paper and pen for working out your exact instructions

## Instructions:

Sit comfortably in a quiet place where you will not be disturbed. If you incorporate circle-casting into your practice, do so before sitting down.

Spend some time thinking about your goal, and visualizing what your life will look and feel like once it has been met. It can be helpful to do some free-writing about this, especially if it's something you have strong emotions about.

Once you feel you have a solid sense of what you want to achieve, write it down in a clear, simple sentence in the form of a command. For example, you can say "Manifest the arrival of my next romantic interest."

Light the candle and center yourself.

Visualize a glowing ball of pure, white light and feel its positive energy harmonizing with you, bringing you into alignment with a feeling of well-being.

Now, the ball begins to spin slowly, and takes the shape of a being composed of pure white light. This shape may

determine itself in your third eye, or you can assign it a shape — butterflies and birds are particularly helpful, or any animal you feel personal kinship with.

Visualize your "thought being" sitting across from you in a tranquil, sunlit space. After a moment or two, communicate with it in the following manner:

- Thank it for arising from your creative source as a defined entity.
- Give it its instructions in the form of your command sentence.
- Stipulate that it carry out the work with harm to none.
- **Say** "you have the power of the Universe to draw upon and thus unlimited energy and capacity to carry out this task."
- Instruct it to dissolve and return to formless Universal energy after the goal is accomplished, or after 7 days, whichever comes first.

Now, visualize the glowing thought form leaving your space in whatever manner is most appropriate for you. For example, if it takes the shape of a butterfly, it can flutter out the window or even out through the ceiling.

Finally, seal the work by saying **"It is done,"** or other affirming words of your choice.

## Ritual and Spell Basics

There are, quite literally, millions of spells. That might actually be a low number, depending on how distinct each spell needs to be.

Most involve herbs, crystals, or stones. The spells in this book do occasionally call for additional items. But each additional item is just an extra that helps set the tone of a spell or more finely focus its energy. The spells and rituals can be performed without anything extra at all. But the one thing they cannot function without is the magic of the Moon.

Before diving into the magic itself, it is important that practitioners understand the difference between rituals and spells. Rituals are rites during which Wiccans honor the Moon, the Goddess, and Her energy. There are several different kinds of rituals for each phase of the Moon. This book focuses on one piece.

Spells, on the other hand, are meant to tap into the energy of the Moon and use it to enact the will of the magic use. It is possible to honor the Goddess and the Moon while doing this, of course. But honoring the source of the energy is not the main intent of a spell.

It is also important to note that practitioners should only do spells and rituals they are comfortable with. Some practitioners prefer to perform their work Sky clad. Or, in other words, nude.

Other practitioners practice certain rites from the very beginning of Wicca such as the Five Fold Kiss.

None of this is required, however. Practitioners do not have to engage in rituals or spells that make them uncomfortable in any way. It does not matter if the discomfort stems from as aspect of the rite or from the rite as a whole.

Wicca is a religion that connects the individual to nature and the Divine. There is no reason that discomfort need be a part of that.

The spells and rituals in this book are meant to be largely accessible to most people. They are written for solitary practitioners but can easily be adapted to fit groups of magic users, which are sometimes known as covens. The only steadfast requirement is that they must be performed during the appropriate phase of the Moon or lunar event. Otherwise they may not work or, if they do work, they may create unintended outcomes.

Each ritual listed below begins with an outline for a ritual bath that includes some herbs, potential candles scents and colors, as well as a chant or short song that practitioners can sing while bathing.

The ritual then moves into ideal ritual clothing as well as a few alternatives. The clothing is largely gender neutral as robes and tunics have been through much of early history. Each description then moves into the ritual itself, followed by steps to take once the rite is completed. And,

finally, each section is rounded out with spells that are ideal for each phase of the Moon.

Although each component of the ritual can be fine-tuned or – in many cases – dropped altogether, there are specific reasons each step has been included. From ritual bathing to cleaning up afterward, practitioners are advised to at least understand the purpose of a step before they alter the rituals from their presented formats.

Preparing for After the Ritual

Rituals and spell work require a lot of energy. Some people can channel or offer this energy with absolutely no concerns. They come out the other side of a rite feeling refreshed and blessed. Some people, on the other hand, come out feeling drained. It all depends on how a magic user relates to their own energy.

Regardless of which category a magic user falls into, they should expect to come out of a ritual needing food, water, and rest. Even people who find rites energizing may come across one that leaves them more exhausted than usual. It is always a good idea to have snacks and drinks waiting for everyone who participates in a rite.

Though some groups suggest alcohol, as it is a traditional celebratory drink, this is not required. Water is ideal, as many magic users find themselves parched after the exertion of a rite.

Other good options are fruit juices, flavored waters, and teas. Artificial drinks are less popular, as they belong more to the mundane world and less to a world where humans connect deeply with nature.

Ideal snacks for post-ritual fuel include nuts, fruit slices, and cut vegetables. If the ritual is particularly important, such as for a holiday, personal celebration, or rare lunar occurrence, some Wiccans prefer to have whole meals waiting.

Whichever route a practitioner takes should keep in mind the idea of staying connected with the world around them. And, as the ritual is meant to honor the Divine, refreshments after the ritual should honor the practitioners. This means opting for healthier options and ensuring there is something for everyone, regardless of dietary restrictions.

Ritual Bathing

Not all practitioners perform ritual baths. The concept may be new even to experienced magic users. But it is an ancient concept that spans multiple cultures and magical practices.

At the base level, a ritual bath is a way for magic users to get themselves into the right frame of mind. Even if they bathed only that morning, a ritual bath changes the tone of their energies.

They leave behind the stress and pressures of their mundane day. In their stead, practitioners can accept the calm, purposeful energy they will need during a ritual.

Ritual baths also help magic users wash away any unwanted energy. Everyone picks up stray bits of energy throughout the day, some good and some bad. And, for the most part, that energy remains part of people until they next ground, center, or bathe. Magic users shake this energy off more readily because they know how to handle it. But a ritual bath helps them clear out unwanted energy much more easily.

And though it is called a ritual bath, many practitioners who engage in this step prefer to take a ritual shower. "Ritual bath" just has a more esoteric ring to it for most people. And though the reason for the name change might be a bit silly, the purpose of a shower versus a bath is not.

When most people bathe, they do it in a small tub of standing water. That water is derived from pipes in their home and is not rooted in a natural source that can cleanse the water as they bathe.

Few people have access to a clean body of water in which to wash away errant energy. Ritual baths in a standard bathtub would remove energy from the practitioner, of course.

But the energy would just stay in the water until the practitioner drained the tub. At that point, much of the energy would just reattach itself to the magic user.

Showers, on the other hand, wash all the unwanted energy down the drain. Rather than swirling around the person only to reattach, errant energy is swept away before it can find its way back to the magic user. It also helps that these showers wash away the dirt and grime of a day in the mundane world, leaving the magic user feeling refreshed for their ritual.

Ritual bathing does not stop at the shower itself. Many practitioners take it a step further by continuing their chant or mindful self-awareness while they apply lotions, fix their hair, and – in some cases – apply makeup. Most people continue this focus into the next step, which is putting on ritual clothing, also known as ritual garb.

## Ritual Garb

Most people have seen movies with magic users in them. Each movie involves long cloaks, hooded robes, and maybe even some sort of slipper. These costumes give the magic users the aura of medieval monks calling on powers greater than they truly understand in order to work some unseen or unknowable purpose.

While actual ritual garb lacks much of pop culture's melodrama, there are a few things that costume designers get right. Most ritual garb is based on the style and clothing of pre-Christian Britain and Ireland. This is slowly changing, however, as practitioners with more diverse heritages join the religion and more people create their own version of Neo-Wicca.

Before a Wiccan can design their own ritual garb, however, it is important that they understand the basic requirements for such clothing. These requirements, as well as the cultural roots of Wicca, have shaped what is now known as traditional Wiccan ritual garb.

The most important aspect of ritual clothing is that it is comfortable. It shouldn't be too tight or cut poorly. And the material should be comfortable against the practitioner's skin.

Uncomfortable ritual clothing will only serve to distract the magic user. At best, this will interrupt their ability to properly honor the being at the center of their ritual. At worst, this can cause a spell to lose power or go astray.

Ritual garb must also be safe. This means that, while flowing robes are popular, sleeves should be relatively snug against the wrists and arms so they do not dip into a candle flame accidentally.

A robe's hem should also be an inch or so above the ground so that practitioners don't trip on it when moving around during a ritual.

Safety is just as important when selecting footwear for a ritual. If the ritual is held indoors or on soft grass inside the bounds of private property, magic users can go barefoot or opt for soft-bottom slippers.

If the ritual is held outdoors, particularly on land that other people have used, hard-bottom shoes are recommended. Rituals performed in the woods almost always require boots or modern shoes to protect the wearer's feet from rocks, sharps sticks, and any garbage other people might have left behind.

And while most ritual garb is made to resemble clothing from bygone eras, it is entirely possible to wear modern clothing for rituals. If a magic user chooses to go this route, they should set aside an outfit that is solely for ritual use. This prevents the clothing from picking up any errant energy and ensures that the clothing is always clean when it is time for rituals.

And, on that note, it is important to keep ritual clothing clean.

If something spills on a ritual garment, it should be cleaned up right away. Stains not only make the garment seem less important, but they can carry energy from one ritual into another.

Practitioners who want to make their own ritual garb should start simple and work their way up to more complex garments and decorations. It is perfectly acceptable to start with a "street clothes" outfit with only a few

pieces of ritual jewelry, then slowly substitute handmade alternatives.

Practitioners do not need to have a lifelong ritual outfit ready before their first ritual. They can start with what they have and change things as the need and possibility arises.

Wiccans who perform a lot of rituals or for whom religion is a central pillar of their lives may have specific clothing for each type of ritual.

The ritual garb subheadings for each ritual will include suggestions for every level mentioned above. From those who wear street clothes and simply need a small trinket to those who have clothing specific to each ritual.

## Creating a Circle

Once the practitioner is ready to begin their ritual, they must cast a protective circle. These are energetic barriers that protect a magic user from outside energy – and keep their own energy focused on the ritual – until they have completed their rite. They are raised at the beginning of any spell or ritual, then are released as the last act of the rite.

There are several ways to cast a protective circle. Some practitioners choose to etch a permanent circle into the floor where whey perform spells and rituals.

Others prefer to use a large loop of string that can be laid out before a rite and collected up afterward. Still others use material like salt or chalk to create a temporary and disposable circle. And yet others rely solely on visualization.

Each variation on the circle has its pros and cons. Most Wiccans choose the version that works best to suit their needs. They consider whether or not they can practice openly, how much space they have, where the practice, and how often they are likely to perform a rite.

With these criteria in mind, they decide which circle marking technique best suits their needs and they practice it until they are adept at raising their energy.

Protective circles should be large enough to encompass all magic users involved in a ritual or spell, a central altar, and any markers used to indicate the cardinal directions.

Regardless of the material used to lay the circle – or if the circle is made using visualization alone – practitioners should walk the inner perimeter of their circle before raising its energy.

This should be done in a clockwise direction, which is also known as Deosil. Walking in this direction puts the magic user more in tune with the energy of the Earth, as it is the same direction that the Sun travels through the sky each day.

Once the outline has been placed around all of these components, the person in charge of the ritual closes their eyes and visualizes the circle as a ring of energy. They then imagine this circle becoming a sphere, closing the ritual in on all sides and protecting those within from harm.

No energy can pass back and forth across the barrier unless it is invited. A physical being can cross the circle, however, and this may break the energetic barrier.

For this reason, it is important that anyone participating in a spell or ritual should stay inside the circle from start to finish unless there is an emergency. In this case, if only one person needs to leave, the practitioner leading the ritual can create a door by which the person can leave. If everyone needs to leave, the leaders can drop the magical barrier, releasing all the energy at once.

Bugs and pets can also break the shield of a protective circle but it is not as easy for them to do, since they carry less energy than a human. Still, if possible, practitioners should keep their pets in a separate area from their ritual space.

This will prevent any unintentional breaks in the circle and allow the ritual or spell to be completed in peace.

Some practitioners use chants to focus their energy while they raise their circles. Each ritual in this book includes its own specialty chant for those who wish to use them.

Spells, on the other hand, rarely require chants since the protective circle is often smaller and containing lower energy levels. Magic users can raise circles in these instances much more easily, so no chants have been written for the included spells.

## Calling the Quarters

As the Moon and sun are important in Wicca, so are the four cardinal directions. North, south, east, and west are often referred to as the Four Quarters or the Four Watchtowers.

They are called before every ritual or spell so that their energy can support whatever work the magic user wants to do. Then, at the end of the rite, the energy is released before the protective circle is lowered.

Unlike most energy, the energy of the Watchtowers is neutral and so is not stopped by things like protective circles.

Not only do each of the directions have their own energies, but they have elements that they alone relate to. North is the direction of Earth, the most stable of the elements. It is strong, subdued, and sturdy. South, conversely, is fire. It is bright and hot, energetic and chaotic. East represents air, which is the softest of the elements.

It easily changes direction, carries only that which is light as a feather, and brings breath to every lung though it is the most intangible of the elements. Finally, there is west, the watchtower of water. Water, too, can change direction.

But it usually takes more time, particularly deep water. Water changes and shapes things gradually, and can carry just about anything if respected.

Each element connects to the phases of the Moon and the faces of the Triple Goddess in its own way. Because of this, the incantations used to summon the Watchtowers tend to change from ritual to ritual depending on the phase of the Moon being honored.

Spells are a little more lenient, since the Moon is aiding the spell rather than the focal point of it. As such, a general call to each Watchtower will suffice, regardless of the Moon's phase.

## Performing the Ritual

The majority of energy in a ritual or spell is used in the core performance. In rituals, it is used to when interacting with the energy of the being honored.

When casting a spell, the energy it put into the spell itself, sort of like fuel being added to a car. It is the thing that makes the spell go. Because each spell and ritual are a little bit different, the details will only be given in the subsections dedicated to each ritual or the selection of spells.

Many of them follow a standard format, which is intentional. Having consistent formats for spells and rituals allows practitioners to learn the framework by heart. Once they do this, they can move within that framework without thinking, allowing them to devote more energy and attention to the ritual itself.

Practitioners new to magic are advised to follow the rituals as they are laid out in this book. Because these rituals were developed by an experienced magic user, they effectively utilize as much energy as possible.

As practitioners gain more experience and confidence with their energy and their magic, they can change things as they see fit. If part of a ritual is not possible due to personal limitations, whether they be space or capability, small modifications are absolutely acceptable. Just be sure that the changes honor the flow and pace of the ritual.

## Ending the Ritual

As energy is called into a protective circle at the beginning of a ritual, so it must be released at the end. This is usually done by thanking whatever entity is being honored – in this case, various phases of the Moon and their corresponding aspects of the Triple Goddess – and then bidding them farewell.

From there, the magic user moves to the Watchtowers. They release these energies in the reverse order they were summoned. If, for example, the practitioner summoned the energies of the Watchtowers in the order of north, east, south, and west, they would release the energies starting with west and working backward through the list.

This allows the practitioner to move in a counterclockwise direction, otherwise known as Widdershins. Though this direction is considered unlucky in some situations, it is simply a way to balance the energy of a ritual. It functions as a way to "unwind" the energy that the practitioner "wound up" by walking Deosil at the beginning of the ritual

## Cleaning Up

The Wiccan appreciate for balance and a sense of connection goes beyond the metaphysical and metaphorical.

Wicca encourages both of these traits while also focusing on a sense of personal responsibility, all of which is particularly important for those who perform magical works. And this is why it is vital that all magic users clean up when they are done with a ritual.

Because each ritual is different, the cleanup will always look a little different. If a ritual call for a practitioner to put something on their altar, there is no reason to take the item down unless that's what the practitioner wants to do. Similarly, if a magic user drew a chalk circle on their floor and it is safe for them to leave it in place, they don't have to wipe it away when the ritual is over.

Many rituals involve things like flowers, herbs, and food. And though some practitioners enjoy leaving these things on their altar as offerings to the Goddess and the God, they can quickly sour.

If someone chooses to leave offerings on their altar, they should check on those offerings a few times a day to make sure that no bugs or rot have set in. At that point the Divine beings have taken all the energy they want or need from the offering.

It is safe to dispose of it as any other plant waste. Cleaning up after a ritual is especially important if it was held outdoors. Even dried plants can drop seeds that may or may not be invasive to the area.

Animals may get into offerings of food that then make the animals sick. And it goes without saying that no member of a religion focused on nature worship should be comfortable littering.

If the practitioner is wearing ritual garb, now is the time to take it off. They should do so slowly and with focused intent.

As they do this, they should also feel for any differences in the energy of the garment from when it was put on. If there are vast differences or if the garment feels heavy or dirty, it may need to be laundered and cleansed before it is worn again.

Cleansing is usually a simple affair in which Wiccans leave items out in the light of a full Moon so that all unwanted energy can be washed away.

# Various Other Helpful Spells

There are some spells that are going to be helpful to you but do not necessarily fall into a specific category. This is where these spells are going to be located.

Finding what has been lost

It does not matter how long or short your spell is, if you put your entire heart into it then it is going to bring you the results that you are looking for.

With this spell, you are going to be trying to locate something that you may have misplaced in your home.

What you need

- A white candle

What to do

- Light your candle and place it on something that is going to make it easy to carry around without dropping it.

- Walk room to room saying this incantation

I need what I seek

Give me a peek

Draw my eyes

For my prize

- As you go into a room and say your incantation, look around the room so you can see if you are feeling drawn to where the object may be located.

## Hushed moment

Whenever some peace is needed in your life so that you are able to smooth out what is happening around you, this spells is one that you can use.

What you need

- White thread (several inches long)

- White feather (1)

What to do

- You need a quiet place to do this spell, even if that means that you lock yourself in the bathroom to do it.

- With the thread, tie the feather to it, but do not use all of the string for this.

- Hold the end that is not holding the feather and place the feather in front of your face.

- Breath out and watch as the feather swings until it comes to rest

- As the feather is swinging, whisper these words

Still, quiet, hush

I am not in a rush

- You are going to repeat your spell once against after the feather has come to rest

# **Calming spell**

It is hard to calm down once you have gotten yourself worked up or if you just feel as if you need a little bit of support. With this spell, you are going to be able to find the calm that you need.

What you need

- Noise of some kind of keep you calm (or silence if you prefer)

- Crystal (amethyst is good for calming rituals)

- A bowl filled with water

- A candle (color choice is yours)

- Incense or oil in a scent that is appealing to you

What to do

- Light your candle along with your incense if you are using some.

- Ensure there is clean water in your bowl before placing your crystal in it.

- Work towards clearing your mind of the chaotic thoughts that may be swirling around your head and focus on positive calming thoughts.

- Once you have control of your thoughts, project your calmness to the water so that it may absorb that calming energy.

- At the point in time that you feel like you have gotten enough calming energy into the crystal that you are using, you will remove the crystal from the water.

- If you have picked to use oils, dab a little bit of oil on your rock. If you are using incense, hold your rock over the smoke so that it may absorb the smell that you associate with being calm.

- The last thing you do is hold your crystal over the flame of your candle in order for it to dry.

- Keep your crystal with you, and at any point in time, you begin to feel anxious you can hold it or rub it in order to feel the calm energy that was absorbed into it through your ritual.

## **Full body blessing**

In doing this spell, you are going to be connecting your physical body to your spirit as well as opening up your readiness channel. You are going to want to do this during a full moon outside so that you can see the moon.

What you need

- Pine incense

- White candle

- Sandalwood incense

- Bowl of water

- Pinch of salt

What to do

- Light your candle and incense

- Sprinkle the salt into the water

- Standing at your altar, you will touch each part of your body saying the following:

Eyes: bless my eyes that I might have clarity of vision

Mouth: **bless my mouth that I may speak the truth**

Ears: **bless my ears that I may hear all that is spoken and not**

Heart: **bless my heart that I may be filled with love**

Feet: **bless my feet that I may find and walk my own true path**

- Allow yourself to be filled with understanding and love that is being offered from the Goddess

- After you are done, you will extinguish your candle and let your incense burn down. You will want to dump the water into the earth so that any negative energy it may have captured is released back into the earth.

## Wand blessing

A wand is not a required tool for doing your spells and rituals. However, it is something that you may decide to use from time to time. If you decide to use a wand, you are going to want to bless it so that it can be blessed and charged so it is ready for its intended purpose.

What you need

- Your wand

What to do

- Holding your wand, say the following incantation

**Through the strength of the elements**

**Light of the sun, empower this wand.**

**Splendor of fire, empower this wand.**

**Speed of lighting, empower this wand.**

**Swiftness of wind, empower this wand.**

**Depth of the seas, empower this wand.**

**Stability of the earth, empower this wand.**

**Firmness of rock, empower this wand.**

I charge and empower this wand.

So mote it be.

# Wiccan Clothing And Ritual Attire

Many hopeful Wiccans wind up pondering whether there's hugely a "clothing regulation" for taking an interest in formal rituals. Much has been made of the practice of working "skyclad," or naked, in Wiccan covens. While the facts confirm that the first Gardnerian type of Witchcraft included ritual nakedness and that numerous conventional covens still pursue this practice, skyclad is surely not by any means the only choice. Today there are numerous inventive, mixed ways to deal with Wiccan clothing and gems, as you will see beneath.

If you're trying to join a coven or a casual Wiccan circle, you'll need to discover what their conventions are as far as ritual attire (if any) and decide to what you're OK with. If you're a singular Wiccan, you don't have to check with anybody, however yourself when it comes to what you'll wear during the ritual. If you pursue a custom that calls for working skyclad as alone and you're alright with it, by all methods do! Else, you might need to consider some other normal choices utilized by covens, circles, and solitaries the same.

ROBES, CLOAKS, AND OTHER POSSIBILITIES

COMMON WICCAN CLOTHING ITEMS

Wiccans and different Pagans regularly wear ritual robes as a way of isolating themselves from the ordinary commonplace parts of life and upgrading their feeling of en

chantment and riddle. For these professionals, wearing a robe is as much a piece of the psychological and spiritual arrangement for ritual as cleaning up or sitting in contemplation. Regularly Wiccans wear nothing underneath their ritual robes, yet this is a personal decision — as always, do what's agreeable for you.

Robes can be acquired or high quality — you can discover straightforward examples online regardless of whether you're not an accomplished sewer — and are accessible in pretty much every shading possible. Irrespective of whether you're purchasing or sewing, notwithstanding, make sure to focus on a significant thought: combustibility. There are some intricate and streaming robe structures out there that ought not to be worn anyplace close to light fire, particularly if there's a breeze!

A few professionals want to wear a shroud during the ritual, especially if it's being held outside. These can be put on over ritual robes or normal clothing, however, are commonly not worn without anyone else since they generally affix at the neck. Contingent upon how to expand the structure, shrouds could conceivably have hoods as well as sleeves. Similarly, as with robes, you can discover a lot of pre-made shrouds on the web, or make your own. You could likewise do some chasing around at vintage shops and repurpose an old article of clothing into your ritual shroud!

There's no need, be that as it may, to make or buy unique Wiccan clothing for your ritual work if you're a single

professional. A lot of Wiccans wear something that is as of now significant to them—a most loved flowy dress or shirt, an all-dark group, or some different bits of clothing that has a different reverberation.

## WICCAN JEWELRY

Notwithstanding, or even rather than, exceptional clothing, numerous Wiccans will wear at least one bits of magical gems during ritual and spellwork. This may incorporate a pentacle or other magical image on a string or chain around the neck; precious stone-studded rings, armlets, anklets or pieces of jewelry; or even a diamond-encrusted headpiece. Anything that you feel upgrades your energy is a decent decision.

It's ideal for accusing these bits of your power to get the perfect impact. If you charge them well, with enough engaged aim, you will probably feel a slight "buzz" of energy when you put them on.

# Conclusion

Many people, when presented with the ideas surrounding the Law of Attraction for the first time, will feel excited and daunted all at once.

It's wonderful to know that we can shape our lives just by changing the way we think. Yet it's incredibly difficult, at least at first, for most of us to change how we think! So where should you even start?

The sources listed on the "Suggestions for Further Reading" page below contain further concepts, strategies and practices that can help you take what you've learned in this guide to the next level. You'll also find a few sources that can help you broaden your exploration of Witchcraft and magic, if you so desire.

But no matter what you choose as your next step, it's worth keeping in mind that you can't force a new abstract concept like the Law of Attraction to become a solid and complete framework for your life experience right away.

Integrating a new belief takes time and patience. Most importantly, it requires the practice of paying attention to the way your mind works.

As you do so, you'll identify opportunities to shift habits of thought, releasing those that no longer serve you on your path and making room for new habits that will ultimately change the way you experience the world.

This process takes different forms and occurs at a different pace for each individual, but no matter how you approach the work of changing how you think, the main thing to keep in mind is that you **can** choose where to put your mental energy.

And even when you find yourself unintentionally falling back into old habits of thought, remember that each day is a new opportunity to make a new choice that will lead you in the direction you want to go.

Keep reaching for the better choices, and you'll see new manifestations develop in your life that feel—no matter what your spiritual orientation—just like magic.

www.ingramcontent.com/pod-product-compliance
Lightning Source LLC
Chambersburg PA
CBHW081422080526
44589CB00016B/2633